Titles in the series *Unesco manuals for libraries:*

Titles in this series:

The organization of intermediate records storage

by A. W. Mabbs
with the collaboration of Guy Duboscq

Unesco   Paris 1974

Published by the United Nations
Educational, Scientific and Cultural Organization
7 Place de Fontenoy, 75700 Paris

Printed by Arts Graphiques Coop Suisse, Basle

ISBN 92-3-101152-9
French edition: 92-3-201152-2

Preface

During the past three decades the function of records management has been integrated into national archives services; it is now recognized as an essential task of the archivist. Both administrators and archivists had become aware that the enormous growth in the number of records produced by modern public administration required joint action to establish an effective mechanism of control as an indispensable prerequisite for administration and for research. With this common aim in mind, both sides met in a joint effort which eventually led to the creation of records management systems in several countries.

While these systems vary in some aspects from country to country, they have been gradually developed and consolidated. Their most important function is to provide for intermediate storage of records; i.e. to ensure preservation of public records no longer currently used by the administration, which have to be stored temporarily while they are re-arranged, evaluated and selected for either destruction or permanent archival preservation for research.

The methods and techniques of that intermediate storage are the theme of the present manual which is the outcome of a contract between Unesco and the International Council on Archives.

The manual, which is intended for leading administrators and archivists, has been prepared by A. W. Mabbs, Records Administration Officer of the Public Records, London, in collaboration with Guy Duboscq, Director-General of the Archives de France.

Mr Duboscq has written a companion volume in French under the title *Organisation du préarchivage*. The two texts are complementary, one dealing with the subject from the point of view of countries following the Anglo-Saxon methods, the other from the point of view of countries following French methods.

The opinions expressed by the author are not necessarily those of Unesco.

Contents

Introduction

During the past thirty or more years both archivists and administrators in many countries have become increasingly concerned with the problems presented by the bulk and complexity of records created by modern administrative organizations. In particular, national and other public archives, once the passive recipients of documents no longer needed for administrative purposes, have acquired greater responsibilities for the control of documentation at its source. The extent and nature of this involvement by public archival authorities in records management matters varies considerably. In a few countries, such as the United States of America and Canada, records management policies and procedures affecting public records cover a very wide range, even affecting decisions on the form in which records are created. In others, the public archives is concerned mainly with more limited procedures which are aimed primarily at solving problems of storage, selection and disposal, and at ensuring a regular flow to the Archives of those records which have permanent value.

In spite of considerable differences between countries in the law and custom regulating the activities of public archival authorities, in the governmental organization in various countries, in record-keeping practices, and in the quantities of records to be dealt with, it is possible to state the common aims of archivists in approaching problems of modern records; to intervene in some way and at some stage in record-keeping matters in government and other public bodies, particularly in order to ensure the preservation of records which will be required for historical and other research, while allowing the systematic destruction of all other records at the earliest possible time after administrative use has ceased.

Most countries, even those with limited experience in records management matters, believe that effective control of records is possible only if sufficient account is taken of the need to provide adequate storage facilities for papers during the time they are still in use by the organizations which have created them. Even if papers of the more ephemeral kinds are systematically eliminated as soon as their use has ceased, there remain large quantities of papers which have to be kept for longer periods, even though most of them will eventually be destroyed. The generally accepted solution is for the public archival authority to provide intermediate storage of the kind which has come to be known as the records centre.

The use of records centres, as part of a general system of records management, is now well established in a number of larger and smaller countries; and their use is widely accepted as desirable or essential in many other countries. For this reason Unesco has thought it desirable to publish at the present time this manual, which is intended to give some general guidance, based on the experience of a number of countries, on the principles and practice of records centre usage.

Before attempting to write the manual the authors, Guy Duboscq, Director-General of the Archives of France, and A.W. Mabbs, Records Administration Officer of the Public Record Office in London, who were assisted by Michel Duchein, Conservateur en Chef at the Direction des Archives, Paris, conducted an inquiry among the public archival authorities of a number of countries.[1] Replies were received from the following: Austria, Belgium, Bulgaria, Canada, Czechoslovakia, Denmark, Finland, France, Federal Republic of Germany, German Democratic Republic, Hungary, Israel, Italy, Malaysia, Madagascar, Nigeria, Norway, Netherlands, Poland, Romania, Sweden, Switzerland, Union of Soviet Socialist Republics, United Kingdom, United States of America, and Yugoslavia. The authors wish to thank these countries warmly for the valuable help which they have given.

The two versions of the manual, in English and French, are identical in the general arrangement of chapters; and the broad conclusions and practical criteria adopted by the authors are the same. Differences in terminology, however, have created considerable difficulty in preparing identical texts in both languages. In

1. The text of the questionnaire is printed below as Appendix 1.

particular, the lack of an English equivalent for the word *préarchivage* has created difficulties which go beyond those of translation. *Préarchivage* is defined in the French version as 'the treatment of papers produced by administrative organizations between the time these papers are removed from the offices where they are created to the moment when they are transferred to the historical archives'. Exact translation into English of some of the passages in which there is general discussion of theory of *préarchivage* did not conform sufficiently with the English presentation of the records centre as a component of a wide system of records management.

For these reasons the authors decided not to offer two precisely identical versions in which each is an exact translation of the other. They have chosen instead to prepare parallel texts which present broadly similar principles in terms which will be familiar to English- and French-speaking readers respectively.

General principles of the
records centre:
its use in several countries

THE NEED FOR THE RECORDS CENTRE

The need to provide records centres arises from the very large quantities of documents which are produced by modern administrative organizations, and the necessity to keep them as economically as possible before they can be destroyed or transferred to the Archives.

The extent of the problems presented by the bulk of modern public records can be illustrated by two examples. In 1955, when the United States of America was considering the need for more comprehensive records management, an inquiry showed that departments and agencies of the federal government were holding about 4,500 miles of records. More recently in 1962, the situation in France was similarly investigated, and it was found that over 300 miles of records were held there by departments of central government. In other countries where the problem has been assessed figures of this kind proportionate to the size of the country have been given.

The absence of any systematic policy of storage and disposal of such large quantities of records has led to dangers of different kinds. Archival authorities in some countries have been faced with demands from public departments to take into the Archives large quantities of papers which still retain some administrative use, and which therefore cannot be reduced in quantity by the removal of documents of no historical value. Apart from wider archival objections to this procedure, the high cost of traditional archive repositories does not justify this mis-use of storage space for records of which perhaps only 5 to 10 per cent will be considered worthy of preservation.

13

A more common situation arises from the accumulation in office accommodation of large quantities of papers which have lost most of their administrative use. Even when a controlled system of retirement provides an orderly flow of records to more remote parts of the building in which records are used, storage problems arise when basements and other inferior accommodation become full. In these circumstances records may be removed to even less suitable storage conditions or submitted to uncontrolled destruction.

It is therefore in the interests both of government departments and of the Archives to ensure that the arrangements for controlling retirement and disposal of records includes provision for storage of those which are not in frequent use. The most satisfactory and economic method of providing this intermediate storage is in a conveniently situated records centre, in which the capital and maintenance costs of storing records are low, and the respective needs of the owners of the records and of the Archives can be met by a common service. In Canada and the United States a cost-saving of up to 75 per cent is achieved when inactive records are removed from office accommodation to a records centre; and considerable advantages to the longer term interests of historical research have been achieved.

This solution to the problems of storage and disposal of large quantities of records has been adopted in a number of countries, where buildings have been erected or existing buildings have been adapted for this purpose. In France records centres are known as *depôts de préarchivage;* and in Germany as *Zwischenarchive.* In the early days of development of its intermediate repository, the Public Record Office in London used 'limbo' to describe a repository in which documents awaiting either destruction or permanent preservation are stored.

THE SITUATION IN VARIOUS COUNTRIES

Before discussing further the principles and aims of the records centre it is worth giving a brief summary of the situation in several countries, with both some details of existing records centres and any general principles of dealing with records management matters which those countries have stated.

Belgium

There is no records management organization, and no definition of principles of dealing with modern records was given. Archivists in this country are nevertheless aware of the advantages of allowing the Archives to have some responsibility over public records from the time of their creation until they are systematically destroyed or designated for permanent preservation.

Canada

In 1890 the Ministry of Finance raised for the first time the problem of non-current records; but not until 1945 was a practical system set up. All records management matters are the responsibility of the Records Management Branch of the Public Archives of Canada. This branch, which works in close co-operation with the Historical Branch of the Public Archives (both forming a single archival authority, the Public Archives of Canada, under the control of the Dominion Archivist), has the task of helping and advising ministries and federal agencies in deciding records management policy. The Branch advises, inspects, and trains the staff responsible for records work in government departments.

As a function of its general direction of the management of records it takes considerable quantities of non-current records into centres (at Ottawa, Toronto and Montreal) which are under its control. In this way the storage requirements of departments for non-current records are met, and arrangements for disposal and transfer to the Archives of more valuable material are implemented.

These records management activities are regulated by the Public Records Order, 1966.[1] The main advantages of its policies of records management, including the use of the records centres, are identified as substantial economies of space, equipment and staff; the controlled destruction at the earliest possible date of worthless records; and greater facility to identify records of historical value.

Czechoslovakia

The records centre is defined as an intermediate stage between the

1. The text is in *Archivum*, Vol. XXI, 1971, p. 48–50.

administrative bodies producing records and the Archives; it is a repository where documents are kept temporarily for the use of the organizations which have transferred them. The use of the records centre, where documents are systematically weeded and selected for preservation, makes it possible to effect more frequent and smaller transfers.

There is a records centre for the Ministry of Defence, and one for the Ministry of External Commerce. The National Archives provides a pre-archival service for other government departments within its own building.

No statute or formal regulations of any kind apply to the use of the records centre.

In Slovakia there is no records centre system, but there is an awareness of the advantages of creating procedures for dealing with non-current records and their selection and disposal in an intermediate repository.

France

The principles and techniques involved in the use of intermediate storage were accepted in France later than they were in Canada, the United States and the United Kingdom. So far, there is no statute or other regulation which affects this area of records administration.

However, two new ventures in this field have been undertaken in the last five or six years, one affecting the Archives Nationales (which deals with the archives of ministries and other central government organizations), the other affecting the archives of *départements*.

The first is the creation of a records centre, known as the Cité Interministérielle des Archives, at Fontainebleau, near Paris, which is concerned with non-current records of ministries and departments of central government. Some details of this records centre, at present operating only in temporary buildings, are given in Chapter 2.

In the Archives Départementales records centres have been set up in Lyons, Grenoble and Melun. The two former are concerned with records of the *préfectures* of Rhône and Isère; the latter belongs to the Cité Administrative of the *département* of Seine-et-Marne. Another records centre is planned for the Cité Administrative of the region Rhône-Alpes at Lyons.

The general definition of *préarchivage* is given as the operation which allows the grouping in special repositories of administrative papers which have lost most of their active use, but to which reference must be made occasionally, and which have not yet reached the age at which they can be made available to the public or destroyed.

It is expected that in the course of the next year or so the text of a new archives law, now being prepared, will include statutory provision for *préarchivage*, which is not provided by the present archive legislation based on the decree of 21 July 1936.[1]

Federal Republic of Germany

In 1965 the Federal Republic of Germany set up a repository *(Zwischenarchiv)* at Bad Godesberg, near Bonn, to provide storage for agreed retention periods of records produced by departments of the federal government. In 1970–71 the repository at Bad Godesberg was replaced by a purpose-built centre for intermediate storage at St. Augustin, also near Bonn. This records centre is regarded as an integral part of the Bundesarchiv.

There are also two separate records centres for documents belonging to the Ministry of Defence and the Ministry of Foreign Affairs.

Archivists in the Federal Republic of Germany state the general principle of the use of the records centre as the storage of administrative records for limited periods in a repository which is controlled not by the government department which produced the records but which is an integral part of the federal archives and under the control of archivists. It has the double advantage of centralizing storage and facilitating the management of records which are no longer used frequently by departments of federal government.

These procedures are authorized by the *Kabinettsbeschluss* of 8 January 1958, and of 28 May 1965.[2]

Israel

The principles of records management are based on control of filing procedures and retirement of non-current records. Each government department is expected to have, in conjunction with its registry,

1. The text of this decree is in *Archivum*, Vol. XVII, 1967, p. 154, 155.
2. The text of both decrees is published in *Archivum*, Vol. XVII, 1967, p. 39, 40.

a 'holding station' for storage of non-current records. The main aims of these procedures are to economize on storage space, to control disposal of records no longer needed, to arrange and reference non-current records in a way most suitable for the use of both government departments and Archives, and to ensure selection of material of archival value and to control its transfer to the Archives.

The State Archives sets aside part of its space as an intermediate storage for papers of defunct agencies or organizations too small to have their own records store.

There is no legislation specifically regulating these activities, but the archivist is entitled under the archives law to issue directions which are binding on all government departments.[1]

Italy

Problems of records management have not escaped attention in this country; but at the moment the matter is still in the stage of theoretical study. Records centres are envisaged as repositories in which documents which are less than forty years old (the period prescribed by the statute of 1963 for the transfer of records to the Archives) will be stored.[2]

The existence of these facilities and the consequent centralization of storage, as well as selection and disposal arrangements, are expected to facilitate transfer to the Archives of documents of permanent value.

Malaysia

The National Archives Act 1966[3] which provides the legal authority for records management activities in this country, makes a distinction between 'public records' and 'public archives'. The former are the current and non-current records belonging to government departments and other public bodies; the latter are those which have reached the age of twenty-five years, have been designated as having national or historical value, and have been transferred to the National Archives.

Public records which have ceased to have any administrative use

1. The text is in *Archivum,* Vol. XX, 1970, p. 184–87.
2. The text is in *Archivum,* Vol. XIX, 1969, p. 18–21.
3. The text is in *Archivum,* Vol. XX, 1970, p. 209–12.

are retired to a departmental records store for a time before being transferred to the intermediate repository, called the Records Services Centre, which handles non-current records of all departments and agencies of central government. The intermediate stage provides for a more objective evaluation of non-current records which have not been scheduled for destruction.

Norway

The general rule is that all government departments and other public bodies keep their own records until they are about twenty-five years old, when they transfer to the Archives those which have not been destroyed in accordance with existing rules or by specific agreement with the Archives.

It is the duty of each department, during this period of twenty-five years, to distinguish between current and non-current records for purposes of deciding storage location. Non-current records are usually moved to places which are unsuitable for office and other working space (e.g. basements, etc.) after the 'first review' has taken place when records are about five years old.

There is a records centre for military records only.

Netherlands

A distinction is made in this country between 'current' and 'semi-current' records (both of which are still in the custody of the organizations which create them) and 'dormant' records (which are transferred to archive repositories).

By the Archives Law of 1962[1] 'semi-current' records must be kept by the government department or other public authority responsible for them in proper storage conditions and suitably arranged and classified.

To assist in meeting these objectives each government department has its own intermediate storage accommodation. Transfer from these records stores to the Archives of documents which must be kept permanently takes place when they are fifty years old.

The opinion is expressed that a system of *préarchivage*, with records centres providing a common service throughout government, is

1. The text is in *Archivum*, Vol. XIX, 1969, p. 52–68.

excellent in principle, but that it is difficult in practice to achieve satisfactory results owing to lack of adequate resources.

Poland

There are no records centres in this country; but each government organization has its own departmental records stores in which it provides services which are similar to those which would be available in a central records centre. In such departmental records stores non-current documents are kept, valueless papers are destroyed after agreed periods, and transfer of the remainder to the Archives is effected.

Papers are considered to progress through the 'administrative age' to the 'historical age' while kept in these departmental stores. During the 'administrative age' the Director-General of the State Archives has control over records in the departmental archives.

Romania

As in Poland, there are no records centres, but legislation and archival regulations make it the duty of central government bodies and local authorities to establish departmental records stores under their own charge. Records in these repositories are arranged, listed and selected for preservation by specialized staff under the direction of the State Archives.

Sweden

Documents are classified into two categories, according to their age: administrative and historical. The general archive regulations impose on government departments and other public bodies the duty of arranging their documents and reviewing them under the control of the National Archives.

Switzerland

In this country *préarchivage* is defined as an operation which allows the archivist to take into his charge documents produced by government departments and other organizations from the time when they cease to have administrative use, and to service and process them before either transferring them to the Archives or destroying them.

The procedures by which this is achieved are governed by directives from the Federal Archives, approved by the Department of the Interior, which came into force on 1 July 1970.

The advantages of the existing procedures are seen as follows: the establishment of close and continuing co-operation between agency and archivist; the saving of space in offices and local record stores by clearing out papers no longer required for current use; the co-ordination of transfer arrangements; the improvement of records management standards; the more economical storage of large quantities of records of temporary value; the ability to keep records in their proper order and to preserve their integrity; the ability to select records for preservation by currently accepted criteria; the ability to provide an efficient reference service to government departments, and to answer inquiries from contemporary historians; and ability to ensure that only records worth keeping are transferred to the Federal Archives.

A part of the Federal Archives repository is used for intermediate storage.

United Kingdom

The provision of intermediate storage for records of central government was begun immediately after the Second World War; but it was in 1950 that the Public Record Office established the large 'limbo' repository at Hayes, near London. Its purpose is to provide storage for records of government departments until they can be either destroyed or designated for permanent preservation.

Use of this intermediate repository leads to considerable reduction in the costs of storage, and gives the Public Record Office a greater measure of control of the procedures by which government records of historical value are selected for preservation and the remainder destroyed.

The intermediate repository is regarded by the Public Record Office as a component of the general system by which it exercises its statutory responsibility for supervising and co-ordinating the arrangements made by government departments and other agencies of the United Kingdom Government for selection and disposal of their records. The Public Records Act 1958,[1] which arose from the

1. Text of this statute is in *Archivum*, Vol. XVII, 1967, p. 184–91.

recommendations of the Grigg Committee (1954), does not, however, give specific authority for any of the procedures, including the use of intermediate storage, which have been adopted.

The Scottish Record Office is planning an intermediate repository; and a few local government authorities have already provided storage facilities for non-current records.

United States of America

Records of the federal government which have ceased to be in active administrative use but which have not either attained the prescribed age for destruction, or have not been designated for transfer to the Archives, are transferred to a records centre if they cannot be more economically kept by departments and agencies.

The National Archives and Records Service is responsible for fourteen records centres for federal government records. Two are designated as national records centres; the others are regional records centres, primarily concerned with federal records originating in regions covered by these repositories.

Great importance is attached to this system, which leads to very substantial economies to the tax-payer, estimated at $4.33 for each cubic foot of records transferred. There are also lower cost factors for maintenance and for providing reference services for documents in the centres.

Statutory authority for records management in federal government departments and agencies, including the use of records centres, is given by the Federal Records Act 1950.[1]

This law does not apply to state and other levels of local government; but some of these have set up records centres on similar lines to those which are under the control of the National Archives and Records Service.

Yugoslavia

There is a single records centre for federal archives, and other intermediate repositories for papers of some of the republics and for records of specialized bodies (e.g. various social, political and other organizations).

1. The text is published in *Archivum*, Vol. XXI, 1971, p. 91–3.

The records centre is used as a means of providing an intermediate stage between the period when documents are kept in
administrative buildings and the time they can be kept in the
historical archives; but there is no law or formal regulation con-
cerning this intermediate stage.

The advantages are seen in the facilities which the records centre
provides for better and more secure storage for documents in this
intermediate stage due to the more effective and systematic control
provided by the archival authority. It is regarded also as a means of
avoiding the need to make the records available to research workers
while there remains a need to use them for administrative purposes.

THE AIMS OF A RECORDS CENTRE

It will have been apparent from the above summary that most of
these countries regard the provision of records centres as an essential
part of a system by which the public archives on the one hand and
government departments on the other deal with problems of records
which are not in active use. Some countries give emphasis to different aspects of a records retirement system, and to different
advantages offered by the use of a records centre. There is general
agreement, however, that the main aims of the records centre and
the records management procedures associated with its use are as
follows:

1. To prevent the unnecessary use of space in premises used as offices
   for public departments and other bodies for storage of records
   which are no longer in active use.
2. To prevent the use of the Archives (the 'historical archives') for
   storage of papers which retain sufficient administrative use to
   make impossible the elimination of those which have no value
   for historical research, and which have not yet reached the age
   at which they can be made available.
3. To ensure that records which are no longer in active use are subjected to effective procedures for the identification of those which
   can be destroyed at the end of agreed retention periods, and those
   which should be transferred to the Archives.
4. To provide a service for making the documents stored in a central
   repository (or information taken from those documents) available to the various organizations to which they belong.

5. To effect economies in the cost of storing and servicing records which are not in frequent use by concentrating them in repositories built, equipped and staffed by economical standards.

Some of these aims are achieved in some countries without the provision of records centres. If, however, the bulk of records to be stored and controlled is very large it will usually be found impossible to achieve all these aims without establishing some kind of intermediate storage separate from government offices and from the Archives. In particular, those countries in which records centres have been longest established believe that the very high cost involved in storing inactive records can be reduced only by a retirement system which uses low-cost storage in a records centre. The relative cost of centralized intermediate storage is a most important and convincing argument in favour of the records centre.

A general definition of a records centre may be given as follows: a records centre is a repository, under the control of an archival authority, in which the non-current records of a number of separate administrative organizations are stored and serviced economically, and under a controlled disposal system, until they can be destroyed or transferred to the Archives.

2 Structure and equipment of records centres

The number of records centres needed to deal with records of a public nature in any country will depend largely on the geographical size of the country, and on the kind of governmental system (centralized, federated, etc.) which it employs.

In order to avoid some of the difficulties which are discussed later (see Chapter 3), it is preferable to use a records centre only for papers created in the same kind or level of administrative organizations: papers of the central or federal government, papers of regional or other local government authorities, etc. If records of different kinds of administrative authorities are stored in the same records centre there might arise some risk of conflict of responsibility. Examples are as follows:

In a country of medium geographical size with a centralized government, perhaps the most common case, it is usual and preferable to establish a single centre for the departments of central government. The statutory arrangements which control the public archival authority should give it authority over the records of all those departments. This centralization of records centre facilities in such a country leads to more efficiency and more economy in cost and staff than if several records centres are established; but even in countries with a centralized government there may be sufficient dispersal of major government functions from the administrative capital to justify more than one records centre.

Separate records centres can be provided, when the quantity of paper produced makes it necessary or desirable, for regional and local government authorities.

In a country of large geographical size, with a federal government (for example, the United States of America or Canada), it has been found essential to provide a records centre in or near the federal capital for the main papers of federal government, with others to provide facilities for records created by the activities of federal government departments in other places in the country.

In addition it may be necessary to establish centres for the records of state governments, and even of large city governments. In a country of small or medium size, with a federal government, a single records centre for the whole federal administration may be sufficient. On the other hand, the same arrangements as those described above are suitable for regional or local governments (e.g. federal states, cantons, cities, etc.).

THE NEED FOR PHYSICAL SEPARATION OF A RECORDS CENTRE FROM AN ARCHIVES REPOSITORY

The basic requirements of a record centre can be fully met only when it is quite separate from an archive repository solely devoted to the permanent preservation of documents. This distinction is not always clearly maintained; and some countries, which more recently have begun to provide intermediate storage for non-current records, have set aside part of the Archives for this purpose. It will usually become apparent, however, as such countries become more involved in dealing with the problems presented by the bulk of current documentation, that this is not a satisfactory solution and that the economic and other practical requirements in favour of a records management system which involves the use of the records centre can be met only by providing a separate building for this purpose.

THE SITUATION OF RECORDS CENTRES

The first requirement to be fulfilled is to have the records centre in a place which is on the one hand within reasonable distance of the various offices from which records will be transferred, and on the other not too far from the archive repository which will, at some future date, receive those documents which it is decided to preserve permanently.

The second requirement is that the records centre is in a situation which allows easy and relatively quick communications with the various administrative units whose records will be stored there and which will use its services.

The third requirement is that its position allows fairly easy access by the staff working there, without too much time spent in travelling; and perhaps that it should not be difficult to recruit locally some of the lower-grade staff required to operate the centre.

The fourth requirement is that the site should be free from any external danger of fire, explosion or flooding; and therefore as isolated as possible from other buildings, particularly factories. The situation of the centre should also be as far as possible away from an area with a high degree of atmospheric pollution.

These basic requirements have to be considered together with the various cost factors, particularly that related to land values. In most cases a suitable site has been found in the suburbs of an administrative capital or centre, or a short distance beyond. Examples are Fontainebleau, near Paris; Hayes, near London; St Augustin, near Bonn; Suitland, near Washington. All are within a few miles of the respective capitals, with good road or rail communications.

When choosing a site for a records centre it is also necessary, as in the case of repositories for permanent archives, to take account of the need for future expansion. If the size of the planned accommodation takes account only of immediate needs, it is generally satisfactory to allow for expansion to at least twice the initial size.

NEW OR EXISTING BUILDINGS?

Repositories for intermediate storage which have been established use either existing buildings or purpose-built structures. For example, public archival authorities in Belgium, the United Kingdom and Norway have used existing buildings; Canada, France and the United States have used both new and existing buildings; the Federal Republic of Germany and Malaysia, new buildings.

Those in favour of converting existing buildings base their arguments on the lower capital cost. This is certainly defensible if the building is of a kind which makes it possible to convert and equip it suitably and economically. One of the major obstacles to satisfactory conversion arises from the great weight of papers, and the high structural cost of providing floors capable of taking the heavy load. It is also necessary in most cases to provide offices, reference rooms, sorting rooms, and perhaps rooms for fumigation, photo-copying, conservation work and other services. Rarely is it possible to convert existing buildings so as to make the greatest use of available space for storage of records, and at the same time provide office space and service areas to make for a high degree of operating efficiency.

On the other hand, advocates of purpose-built records centres argue that in designing a new building it is possible to impose on the architect the standards required to ensure good and economical storage with adequate planning of facilities required for handling records and servicing them. Generally speaking substantial economies are likely to be achieved in the longer term.

Above all, one of the main reasons for having records centres i that of economy; it would be pointless to build and equip special repositories for intermediate storage if their cost was as high as that of conventional archive repositories. Therefore less expensive design and construction methods, less expensive storage and other equipment must be sought, provided the security of the documents and the working conditions of the staff are satisfactory.

GENERAL PRINCIPLES AND STANDARDS OF STRUCTURE
AND EQUIPMENT[1]

The general design of the building

In the interests of economy in building and in operating costs it is desirable (provided a sufficient area of land is available, taking account of the need for future expansion) to keep the number of floors as small as possible. No more than three floors—ground floor and two upper levels—are recommended.

A records centre consists of two quite separate parts: the storage or stack area where the documents are kept, and the various working areas (for reception of documents, sorting, reference rooms for

1. An example of more precise standards of design and equipment which have been adopted by a national archival authority (the National Archives and Records Service of the United States) for its own purposes in given as Appendix 4.

use of visiting staff of agencies transferring records, cleaning and fumigation, photocopying, perhaps conservation and binding, and of course offices for management, secretarial and other staff of the records centre). To these must be added garages, boiler house, lavatories, canteen, and possibly a dwelling for a caretaker or custodian.

Working areas, offices and other facilities should be isolated from the storage area in so far as possible, by walls and fire-resistant doors, without undue hindrance to communication between the two parts of the records centre.

The whole building should be of permanent structure, using incombustible materials, and must be designed and equipped to minimize the main dangers which threaten documents: fire, humidity, excessive sunlight, fungus (mildew), insects, rodents, atmospheric pollution and theft.

Size of a records centre

The floor area of each records centre will depend on the quantity of papers which it is expected to store there. Calculation of the repository area which will be needed will be based on the height and kind of racking to be installed, and its distribution (the width of gangways). A rough rule which applies to racking about 7 feet to 7 feet 6 inches high, with average width gangways, is that 1½ linear feet of documents will require about 1 square foot of floor area.

On a similar basis of calculation, a ton weight of documents would need about 100 square feet of floor area.

From 5 to 10 per cent of the total area of the centre should be allowed for offices and working space.

The interior of a large single-storey repository should be divided by fire-break walls, with fire-resistant doors of adequate size, so that the maximum area between external and fire-break walls conforms to local fire regulations.

The storage areas and the racking

The load to be supported by the floors must take account of the weight and distribution of the potential load of documents, and of the racking. With racking of a height of 7 feet 6 inches and average

29

width gangways, 220 lbs per square foot can be regarded as a generous figure for maximum loading. For mobile racking, the potential load is twice as high.

The racking can either stand on the concrete floor on each storey of the building, or it can be a self-supporting system in which the racking on all levels is incorporated in vertical stanchions which also carry the weight of each floor.

The height of racking at each level should not be more than 7 feet 6 inches if it is required to reach the top shelves without using ladders. Some countries, however, have adopted higher racking for the storage of documents in a records centre, where the frequency of need to produce documents from the shelves is low.

The floors between each level should preferably be solid. The use of floors with open metal grids is to be avoided because of the risk of fire spreading and the deposit of dirt and dust from upper to lower levels through the open grids.

The layout of the storage area requires careful planning. Wide aisles or gangways at least 8 feet in width should be provided on all sides of the building to allow free access for the largest equipment envisaged for the conveyance of documents from loading bay to storage location. In buildings with a large floor area, one or more main centre aisles of similar width will be needed. The gangways between rows of racking should be of sufficient width to allow easy access to documents and the passage of any handling equipment which will be used.

If self-supporting racking is used the exterior walls can be as light in structure as building and fire regulations allow, since the load of the floors is taken by the upright stanchions.

Whatever internal structure is adopted, the walls should be as free as possible from windows in order to protect documents from sunlight which causes fading of inks, yellowing of papers and drying-up of bindings. This is particularly important in warm and sunny countries.

The actual shelving should be of the simplest possible kind in order to reduce cost. Metal shelving is of course preferable; and a simple means of adjusting the space between shelving should be provided.

Shelving of the mobile type (i.e. moving on rails or pivoting on hinges) is not recommended for records centres, because of its high cost and limited use. Such types of shelving are acceptable only when the floor area is very limited. They do allow from 30 to 50 per cent more storage space, but their loaded weight is greater than that of standing racking.

Stairways and lifts serving all floors should be encased in shafts lined in fire-proof material and fitted with fire-proof doors. Specialist advice on provision of fire-escapes must be obtained.[1]

Protection of the documents

Protection against sunlight has been mentioned above. Fire precautions, apart from the use of incombustible materials in building, racking, packing containers, etc., include provision of metal conduits for electrical wiring, with both local and general fuses or circuit-breakers. An automatic fire detection system should be fitted, preferably working by detection of smoke rather than heat. The requirements for a fire-fighting system should be examined by specialist fire officers.

Against humidity and resulting fungoid growths it is absolutely essential to maintain a moderate and stable temperature of about 15° to 18°C. In the storage area a stable relative humidity of 55 to 65 per cent is desirable. In tropical countries, with both high humidity and temperature, air-conditioning should be provided if possible; but if the cost prohibits such an installation the repository should at least be fitted with an air-filtration system, with means for absorbing excessive humidity by use of silica gel. Electric dehumidifiers are also available.

Against damage from a high degree of atmospheric pollution, and in particular against attack from sulphur dioxide, it is desirable to filter all incoming air. Such filtration will also serve to stop the entry of flying insects and fungus spores which are in the atmosphere.

Against crawling insects and rodents it is necessary to take particular precautions, particularly in semi-tropical countries. The best protection in such countries is to build on pylons which raise the repository above the ground, and to treat the surrounding soil with suitable insecticides.

Security measures against theft should include the protection of windows by metal grilles, adequate security of doors and an automatic alarm system to supplement normal care-taking arrangements.

1. See Appendix 3, Racking in the Intermediate Repository at Hayes (United Kingdom).

Consideration should be given to any specialist storage requirements to be met either inside the main building, or in a separate building, if controlled temperature and humidity conditions of higher standards are needed (e.g. for film and magnetic tapes).

Working areas

The proportion of space allocated to the working areas will depend on the kinds of services which will be undertaken there; but as a general rule about 5 to 10 per cent of the total area of the building should be reserved for office space and other rooms.

The kinds of working areas to be considered are: a covered bay for loading and unloading vans, with a suitable reception area for handling records on arrival or dispatch; a room for fumigating and cleaning records on arrival; a well-lit room or rooms for sorting and weeding documents, fitted with tables and racking; a search or reference room, which should be well lit and equipped with tables, chairs, etc., mostly for the use of staff from agencies which have transferred documents to the centre; photocopying room; a packing room, and perhaps a room for conservation and rebinding work; offices for records centre staff.

Other needs

Other needs to be considered are: a dwelling for a caretaker, and even a resident senior member of staff of the records centre; garages; rooms for storing stationery, packing materials, etc.; boiler room; an incinerator for burning documents; toilet facilities; staff canteen.

Handling equipment and internal communications

In a records centre there is often a need to handle large quantities of records. Trolleys, with four pivoted wheels, fitted with shelves are preferable. Two-wheel trolleys known as sack barrows are also of some use.

In large centres, conveyor belt systems of the continuous belt or hopper types should be considered, as well as electrically driven trolleys. Heavy-duty fork lift vehicles are useful for moving large quantities of records. Lifts (elevators) should be large enough to take both a trolley and the staff needed to handle it.

A telephone system with adequate external lines and internal extensions is essential to avoid unnecessary loss of time in communication.[1]

AN EXAMPLE OF A NEW RECORDS CENTRE

As an example of a recent design of a records centre some details are given of the Cité Interministérielle des Archives at Fontainebleau, a large and important development in France which is now being built. The Cité Interministérielle des Archives is important by virtue of its size 800,000 linear metres of shelving are to be provided) and the originality of its underground construction.

The site occupies an area of 22 acres at Fontainebleau, about 38 miles from Paris, where the erection of a large building above ground is prohibited. At present the site contains two old buildings which have been converted for the storage of records, and another new temporary building. These three buildings will be used for a further ten years by which time the new underground repository will be completed.

Ten separate storage blocks will be constructed, each containing about 80,000 linear metres of shelving. All the blocks with one exception are identical in size and shape. Each standard block consists of five floors of racking below floor level. Above ground each block will have a large loading bay and a room for packing and for handling waste paper. After papers have been unloaded, and checked, they are taken by lift down to their storage location, where they will remain until requisitioned by the agency which transferred them, or until they are destroyed or sent to the Archives Nationales for permanent preservation.

Communication between adjacent blocks will be below ground at each storage level. A circular driveway allows vans to enter the Cité and unload.

One of the blocks, the first to be constructed, has a different above-ground structure, although it is identical underground. This will contain the administrative offices of the Cité.[2]

1. For the general layout and equipment of a records centre, see Appendix 4, Federal Records Center facility standards.
2. The plan of the Cité Interministérielle des Archives is shown below as Appendix 2.

3 The staffing of records centres

In records centres which have already been established in various countries the staffing situations differ considerably both in numbers and kind of staff employed. These differences are explained largely by the size of the centre, the kind of control exercised by the archival authority, and the nature of operations and the range of services performed in any such repository. The arrangements also depend on whether staff working on documents in a records centre are responsible to the archival authority or to the individual administrative organizations which transfer documents there.

STAFFING ARRANGEMENTS IN SEVERAL COUNTRIES

The following summary of staff employed in records centres in six countries shows the general principles adopted in each case. Direct comparison is made difficult by the different nomenclature used for professional and non-professional grades of comparable status and training.

Canada

The management staff concerned with all three records centres number fourteen. These are not required to be professional archivists, although in the past some have been. The 'records managers' who are responsible for the centres, as well as 117 other staff working there, are employed by the Public Archives.

France

The records centre at Fontainebleau is directed by a *conservateur d'archives*, assisted by a *conservateur-adjoint*. Technical, clerical and maintenance staff is still small in number; ten only. The number will be gradually increased to a considerable extent as building of the Cité progresses. All the staff are employed by the Archives Nationales.

In records centres for the *départements* the staff belongs partly to the Archives Départementales and partly to the local administrative authorities (the Préfecture or Cité Administrative), under the direction of the director of the archives service of the *département*.

Federal Republic of Germany

In the Federal Archives, in Koblenz, a 'first-class' archivist has general responsibility for records management matters. A 'second-class' archivist, with one year of specialist training, is in charge of each of the two records centres (one 'civil' and one 'military').

Other staff number twenty-five, of whom fifteen are in the 'civil' records centre, and ten in the 'military' centre. The latter also employs some soldiers. All the staff, except the soldiers, are employed by the Federal Archives.

Malaysia

The managing staff of the records centre comprises a chief archivist and three assistants. Other staff number twenty-three. All twenty-seven are employed by the National Archives.

United Kingdom

The managing staff at the intermediate repository at Hayes comprises two officers who are on the staff of the Public Record Office, which also employs a small staff for cleaning and moving documents. The total staff working in the repository is over 400, but most of these are employed by the various government departments to work on the records which they have transferred there.

United States of America

The fourteen federal records centres employ approximately 1,370 staff of which less than 5 per cent can be described as management staff. Almost none are professional archivists, even at management level. Apart from a small proportion (less than 1 per cent) who have custodial and other duties, the employees in the centres are for the most part administrators, technicians, clerks and secretaries. The National Archives and Records Service is responsible for all staff in the federal centres.

RECOMMENDATIONS FOR STAFFING

In spite of the different kinds of organization and staffing arrangements in countries with different archival traditions and practices, it is possible to formulate some general guidelines on staff requirements which may be helpful to archival authorities planning records centres.

A records centre for documents of a public nature should be under the direct control of the national or other public archival authority. This is the best means of preventing the proliferation of repositories and of obtaining uniformity in the policy of dealing with storage and disposal problems throughout the whole range of administrative organizations covered by the archival authority.

Each records centre should be directed by a senior officer of the Archives, preferably an archivist with not only traditional archival experience but also with special experience in problems of modern records and in records management techniques.

In some countries with considerable experience in the use of records centres (e.g. Canada and the United States) this kind of professional direction is given from the main Archives. The officers immediately responsible in the records centres for their direction are usually 'records managers' with no conventional archival training.

According to the size of the records centre, and the scope of the services given there, the officer in charge of each records centre should be assisted by a suitable number of professional or non-professional staff.

Other staff in a records centre will be of several kinds depending in number and kind on the requirements of the work to be done there. They will include staff to provide clerical and secretarial services, to move records, to clean and maintain buildings and records, to provide adequate custody, and perhaps photocopying and conservation facilities.

It is the general opinion of countries involved in the use of records centres, and of others at present considering their use, that all staff working in them should be employed by the national or other public archival authority. This is essential if the records centre is to provide not only storage for non-current documents but also the range of other services discussed elsewhere in this manual. Full control and effective management of the centre are only possible by this means; and recruitment and training of suitable staff is made more easy.

It is possible, however, to provide an intermediate repository which may not meet all the aims of the fully developed records centre, in which the staff below management level, or some of them, are employed not by the Archives but by the government departments or other bodies whose records are placed there. Use of a records centre for storage of more active records, which require a frequent reference service based on expertise more readily available in the responsible department, may lead to a decision to employ such staff there. Other reasons of practical convenience or financial necessity may also produce arguments in favour of using departmental staff. In most cases, however, this solution is not considered suitable; and if this method of staffing is unavoidable it is essential that management, secretarial and all common-service staff should belong directly to the Archives.

4   Retirement of documents to a records centre

When deciding the kinds of records which are suitable for deposit in a records centre, and the procedures by which they should be transferred there, it is worth considering a widely accepted theory that defines three stages in the life of papers produced by any organization:

The first stage is that in which records are being used frequently in the course of the current activities of the organization which produced them. Records in this stage are often described as 'current' or 'active'.

The second stage is that in which records have ceased to be used frequently in the course of current activities, but nevertheless retain occasional administrative use. Records in this stage may be described as 'non-current', 'inactive' or 'dormant'.

The third stage is that in which records no longer required for administrative use can be either destroyed or, if they have permanent value, passed to the Archives for permanent preservation.

It is normal for papers in the first stage to be kept in the offices in which they are used, or at least stored in a convenient place close at hand. At this stage only the organization which creates the records and uses them to conduct its current business can be responsible for keeping them and controlling their use.

In most countries public archival authorities have little or no influence over the management of records in this first stage, except in so far as the disposal procedures discussed below cannot be comprehensively applied without consideration of both current and non-current papers. In a few countries, however, and notably

Canada and the United States of America, the national archives have a statutory responsibility to advise public departments and agencies on filing methods, to recommend systems of paperwork management, to train records staff working in departments, and to provide expertise in a wide range of records management activities. This intervention from the time of creation of records has not only led to greater efficiency and economy in record-keeping in government departments, but also is of ultimate benefit to the requirements of the Archives and of historical research.

The transition from the first to second stage is usually gradual; and one of the main objectives of a successful records management system is to determine, in respect of each kind of paper in an organization, the time at which retirement is practicable and desirable. In this second stage papers must still remain within the control of the organizations which created them and are responsible for them; but it is essential that the national archival authority also has some kind of responsibility for the records when they have lost their most active use. The general requirement is for joint action by the organization responsible for the records on the one hand and the Archives on the other to arrange procedures which take account of their respective and common needs and interest.

It is the non-current records in this second stage which are those to be considered for deposit in a records centre.

CONTROL OF RETIREMENT AND DISPOSAL

Effective procedures for the orderly retirement of non-current records, and the elimination at the earliest possible time of those with no further value of any kind, are essential to the interests of both public departments and the Archives. Each organization produces papers of a number of kinds which relate to its own field of activity. The length of time for which any category of papers is needed for business purposes may be as short as a month or as long as fifty or more years. There will also be great variation in the periods for which any of these records will be considered sufficiently active to require their storage close to the place in which they are used. It will be possible to destroy some categories of papers, or transfer them to the Archives, wholly and without any detailed examination; while others will require careful appraisal at some date. If records are to be controlled effectively it is necessary to take all these factors into account and to promulgate, in the form of schedules, appropriate instructions for dealing with the records.

Each government department or other organization should reach agreement with the Archives, taking full account of both their needs, on the instructions to be incorporated into these schedules. Disposal instructions should cover all categories of records, from files containing the highest level of policy matters to documents of the most ephemeral value. The schedules should give the following information:

1. The description of the papers.
2. The period of their retention in the department, with instructions for dealing with the records at the end of that period (for example, removal to a records centre or other intermediate store; destruction; transfer to Archives of the whole, a selection or sample).
3. The period of their retention in a records centre, with instructions for dealing with the records at the end of that period (for example, destruction; transfer to Archives of the whole, a selection or sample).

Schedules of this kind, which are in various forms to meet different systems, are known more commonly as disposal schedules, disposal lists, *tableaux d'éliminables* (or *tableaux de tri*).[1] Most schedules apply specifically to the records of a single organization, but general disposal schedules are prepared in some countries containing instructions for records of the same kind (for example, personal files of staff, and accounting documents) which are found in all departments.

KINDS OF RECORDS SUITABLE FOR STORAGE IN A RECORDS CENTRE

It is clear that not all records which may be described as 'non-current' are suitable for deposit in record centres; and it is necessary therefore to consider the factors which should determine which of them should be moved to intermediate storage. Many records, particularly those with shorter retention periods, will be destroyed without removal from the places in which they were created and

1. See Appendix VI and Appendix VII.

have been used. There may also be special reasons for government departments to retain some records in their own premises for long periods, even for a long time after they have become more or less inactive. In general, the most important factors to be examined when deciding which papers should be moved to a records centre are: (a) the frequency with which records need to be used for current business; (b) the length of the retention period; (c) the cost of moving files to a record centre.

In the United States these three considerations have led to the broad principle that files which are referred to not more than once a month per file-drawer should be transferred to a centre, provided the total cost of moving the records does not exceed the saving in storage costs. In Canada there is a similar rule which relates the frequency of reference to a cubic foot of storage space. Such broad criteria are necessary when planning the use of a records centre and when drawing up disposal schedules; but practical considerations prevailing in particular government departments will make it impossible to adhere rigidly to any such rule.

As far as possible the pattern of transfer of records from agency to records centre should be governed by disposal schedules. It is unlikely, however, that demands on records centre accommodation will be confined to scheduled records. Situations will arise (for example, unforeseen demands on office accommodation, removal of departmental offices to another building, the need to deal with records of a defunct agency) in which a records centre will be asked to accommodate records which do not meet the normal requirements for intermediate storage. The circumstances of each case will decide whether or not it is appropriate to transfer to the records centre. It is essential, however, that when unscheduled records are moved to a centre their retention periods or any other disposal arrangements are decided at the time of transfer. The whole purpose of the records centre is defeated if it is used for uncontrolled 'dumping' of documents.

TRANSFER TO THE RECORDS CENTRE

Records normally transferred to a records centre should be those for which such transfer has been directed in an agreed schedule. No unscheduled records should be transferred there without the previous consent of the officer responsible for the centre. For all kinds of records, scheduled or not, there must be a single procedure for transferring them.

The basis of any transfer procedure will be a standard form (in two or more copies as required) on which the transferring organization gives details of the documents (the originating branch, category of records, covering dates, etc.). The degree of detail required will depend on the nature of the documents and the kind of reference service which the records centre will be asked to provide. In some cases it may be necessary to provide not only more detailed transfer lists but also other means of reference (such as any card indexes used by originating departments to refer to their files) which will be needed to give access to the documents.

In the case of records covered by a disposal schedule the transfer form should contain a reference to that schedule and the agreed retention period and other disposal instructions should be noted.

The regulations for transfer of records to the centre should specify any packing requirements, such as the use of standard boxes or cartons into which records should be placed before removal to a centre. In most countries the cost of transport is borne by the transferring organization. When records arrive at the records centre they should be checked against the details given in the transfer form and inventory.

One copy of the transfer form should be signed by a senior officer of the records centre and returned to the transferring organization as a receipt for the documents.

Immediately after receipt of the documents the records centre staff will, if necessary, clean and fumigate the documents before they are given a reference and moved to their storage location.

5 Treatment of records in a records centre

Documents in a records centre remain the property of the organizations which transferred them there; but it is the responsibility of the records centre to store and safeguard the documents, to make them available on instructions from the transferring organization, and to carry out any necessary weeding and selection before destruction or transfer to the Archives.

It is important that on transfer to the records centre any series or class of documents should be stored in the same order as that in which they were kept before removal. Thus any additional references which the records centre gives to documents transferred there should be strictly related to their original order or arrangement.

MEANS OF REFERENCE TO DOCUMENTS
IN A RECORDS CENTRE

The reference system should provide a simple means of finding documents which are described in the transfer forms or lists. In some records centres it is the practice to allot a reference number to each box or bundle of papers received. In others it is found adequate to relate the original reference or description used by the transferring department to the shelf location of the documents.

The location references of the documents should be entered on the transfer form which gives details of the documents. The copy of the transfer form which is signed and returned to the transferring department should also contain this information.

A second copy of the transfer form, with any associated detailed lists, should be filed in the records centre together with other transfer forms and lists relating to documents belonging to the same organization. This information will be kept in the room where staff will deal with requisitions for documents or requests for information from the owners of the records.

ACCESS TO DOCUMENTS

While papers are stored in a records centre they can be made available normally only to the organization which transferred them. If for any reason the transferring organization is willing to allow access to any of its papers to another organization, or to a private research worker, it must signify its consent in writing to the official in charge of the records centre.

These rules are essential in order to give to organizations using the records centre a guarantee that the confidentiality of their records will be fully safeguarded, and to meet the objections made by some opponents of the records centre system that confidentiality is likely to be breached by a common storage system.

When reference is required to documents stored in a records centre this can be provided in several ways:

When the transferring department needs some information which can be obtained easily from a file, the records centre staff can examine the file and give the required information by telephone or letter.

When a transferring department wants to see any of its papers in its own offices it can requisition them and they can be returned there temporarily. A transport service will be needed between records centre and government offices to return such documents with minimum delay. The records centre should keep a register of documents sent back to departments.

The transferring department might wish to send one of its own staff to consult some of its documents. A room should be made available for reference purposes of this kind. The same room could be used to accommodate any member of the public who may be authorized to examine documents kept in the records centre for research purposes.

The records centre should also be equipped with photocopying apparatus (for example Xerox, or even microfilm cameras) in order to provide copies of documents for the use of departments.

If at any time in the future the cost of such equipment is justified by the need, it might be possible to consider electronic techniques of transmitting facsimiles of documents.

RECORDS IN BULK OR IN DISORDER

Particularly in the early stages of developing a systematic disposal system, cases will arise when it will be necessary to accommodate records which have been stored in bulk and even in total disorder. Sometimes such accumulations of documents are old enough to have no administrative use, and their owners are not prepared to examine them to decide their nature and value. In such cases if the records centre staff insist on obedience to the normal rules and refuse to accept the records, the documents are likely to be destroyed.

It may therefore be advisable for the manager of the records centre, having established that the documents in question are worthy of investigation, to admit them to the centre in the expectation that staff there will be able to sort them and decide which are worthy of preservation.

The experience of more than one country is that, by undertaking the task of sorting and arranging such accumulations, it is possible to demonstrate to an organization the practical value of dealing efficiently with its records, and of having for the future a systematic procedure for transferring records in proper order.

WEEDING AND SELECTION

It was explained in an earlier chapter that as far as possible all documents entering a records centre should be given a retention period at the end of which some predetermined action will be taken to deal with them. These retention periods are set out in disposal schedules which should apply, of course, to the whole range of records in any department and not only to those which will go into a records centre.

Not all categories of scheduled records can be wholly destroyed or passed to the Archives when retention periods have expired. In the case of some documents scheduled for total destruction after a period in a records centre it may be necessary to revise the original judgement of their research value. With the agreement of the transferring organization, the Archives may then wish, for example, to make a selection of those which are considered to be worth keeping, or to keep a small sample of them. It may be necessary, in respect of many other kinds of files in a records centre, to submit them to detailed examination, file by file, after administrative use has ceased.

It is not the purpose of this manual to discuss in detail the methods and procedures used in different countries to determine the value of records, either at the stage of making disposal schedules or when detailed appraisal and selection is required. It can be said briefly, however, that disposal schedules can only be drawn up after joint consultation between the organization responsible for the records and the archival authority. The function of the archivist in disposal and appraisal procedures can be performed either by records centre staff or by the Archives itself. However, if the records centre is to be fully effective the staff there should have full responsibility for implementation of disposal instructions for documents stored there.

LIAISON BETWEEN THE ARCHIVES AND GOVERNMENT DEPARTMENTS

An essential feature of a records management system is effective liaison between the Archives and the various government departments and other organizations producing records.

This is achieved either by having staff of the Archives undertake visits or temporary assignments to departments, or by appointing staff in departments to take special responsibility for records management matters and the arranging of transfers to the records centre or to the Archives.

In France, since about 1950, some archivists from the Archives Nationales have been attached permanently to more important government departments, where their responsibilities in records management matters include the preparation of disposal lists. Since the introduction of *préarchivage* these *missionnaires* have been concerned with arranging transfer to the Cité Interministérielle at Fontainebleau of papers which have passed out of active use.

In the United Kingdom a different system has been used since the Public Records Act of 1958 defined the respective responsibilities of the Public Record Office and government departments. Each department appoints an official, known as a Departmental Records Officer, who is responsible for the general control of records, for the first review of files, for disposal lists, for transfer to the intermediate repository at Hayes, and for the departmental responsibility of final selection of records for permanent preservation. The Departmental Records Officer works in collaboration with an Inspecting Officer from the Public Record Office who visits the department and the intermediate repository from time to time, particularly to participate in the selection of records for preservation.

In other countries different systems are used, according to administrative structures and other factors; but in all cases the essential requirement is for the archival authority to be given a suitable means of direct intervention in the management of departmental records to prevent improper destruction and to ensure the effective use of the records centre.

SUMMARY

1. Papers should be transferred regularly to the records centre by the departments and other bodies which create them according to disposal lists agreed between the latter and the public archives.
2. Papers should be transferred according to procedures laid down by the records centre and, in particular, must be accompanied by a transfer form (in two or more copies, as required) giving details of the records transferred.
3. Records centre staff should check the records against the transfer form, amend the list of records if necessary, and move the records to their storage location.
4. The transferring organization should be sent a signed copy of the transfer form, corrected if necessary, on which will be entered the reference by which the documents can be requisitioned.
5. Records centre staff will be responsible for making documents available to the organization which owns them, or to others if that organization gives its consent.
6. Records centre staff will be responsible, if necessary, for examining files to determine their value.
7. Records centre staff will be responsible for any weeding called for by the disposal schedules and will arrange for the destruction of records at the end of retention periods, after obtaining consent of the transferring department.
8. Records centre staff will arrange transfer to the Archives of records deemed to have permanent value.

6 Elimination of documents in a records centre

PROCEDURES FOR ELIMINATION OF VALUELESS PAPERS

As documents stored in a records centre are the property of the organizations which have transferred them there, it is necessary to obtain their authority before destroying any of them.

With some kinds of documents it is possible for the transferring organization to give advance written authority for the destruction of well-defined categories of papers without further consultation after the agreed retention period has expired. In such cases the records centre will implement destruction without formality. Details of the records destroyed will be sent to the transferring department.

With other kinds of papers it is desirable, even though retention periods have been set out in a schedule, for the records centre to obtain confirmation that the papers may be destroyed when the period has expired. This consultation might take the form of sending to the transferring organization a list of the papers due for disposal, asking for confirmation that the schedule may be implemented. At this stage it might be decided to delay disposal of all or some of the papers for a further period, on grounds that they are still needed for administrative purposes; or on the other hand, the Archives might wish to reconsider the historical value of the papers before proceeding with the disposal instructions.

METHODS OF DESTRUCTION

The destruction of papers can be carried out by several methods. They can be made into bales, or put in sacks, and sold as waste paper; or they can be shredded or burned. If the transferring organization has imposed no special conditions for disposal of worthless papers, the officer in charge of the records centre will decide which is the most suitable method of disposing of papers.

Disposal to a waste-paper merchant is suitable only for the least confidential categories of papers; and even for such papers it is desirable to obtain a written guarantee from the waste-paper merchant that there will be no disclosure of information from the papers before they are pulped. The sale of large quantities of waste paper can be profitable; but in some countries the price of waste paper has diminished considerably during the past twenty or so years. It is sometimes difficult therefore to get rid of waste economically in this way; other means of disposal might then be considered.

Shredding of papers before selling as waste paper is suitable for confidential papers which require special security precautions. Several types of shredding machines are available, details of which need not be given here.

Burning is a means of disposing of secret and confidential papers. As all records centres will have to dispose of some documents in this way, it is necessary for each records centre to have a suitable incinerator installed, separate from the main buildings and with adequate facilities for safeguarding the confidentiality of the documents.

7   Transfer from records centres to the Archives

GENERAL CONSIDERATIONS

It has been emphasized in earlier chapters that while documents are in a records centre they remain the property of the various organizations which transferred them there. When documents which have been selected for permanent preservation are removed to the Archives their status changes. In some countries when papers are transferred to the Archives the department or other body which created them loses all rights in them. For example, in France, at the time of *versement* the documents become the exclusive property of the Direction des Archives. In other countries the organizations transferring records to the Archives retain some kinds of legal responsibility for them; but their original rights must always be considerably limited by the archival laws which give the duty of permanent custody and preservation to the Archives.

The date at which transfer to the Archives takes place will depend largely on the time after which they can be made available to the public. At present the 'closed period' for public records varies from country to country; and documents of some particular kinds will sometimes be made available even before the expiry of the normal closure period. Since the Extraordinary Congress held in Washington in 1966 an increasing number of countries have adopted thirty years as the period after which public records shall be generally made available to the public.

During storage in a records centre, at least until the expiry of the period after which action is instructed in a disposal schedule, documents will have been kept in their original order, and not subjected to reclassification or other procedures. After the specified period of retention in the records centre has expired, and documents for permanent preservation have been isolated and the remainder destroyed, it is then necessary for the permanent records to be classified, listed and catalogued according to whatever archival methods and standards are being applied. These processes and other preparations for making records available can take place either in the records centre or in the Archives after transfer. Depending upon the procedures by which these preparations are made, in any country it is possible to prescribe a general rule for the latest date, before records are due to be opened, by which transfer formalities must be completed.

Difficulties in meeting these theoretical requirements will arise in some countries, particularly in two quite different situations which commonly exist: (a) the Archives may not have sufficient storage space for records awaiting transfer; in this case accumulative delays in the orderly transfer of documents are likely to be detrimental to the interests of historical research; (b) on the other hand, if accommodation in the records centre or other intermediate stores is insufficient to keep all the documents which have to be kept for some years before their administrative use is exhausted, there will be a pressure to transfer to the Archives documents, perhaps not all of permanent value, which will not be open to the public for some time.

It is therefore essential for a public archival authority to develop a long-term policy for the planning and co-ordination of the requirements of both the records centre and the Archives, so that the storage and staffing needs of both are adequately met.

PROCEDURE FOR TRANSFER TO THE ARCHIVES

An example of procedure for transfer of documents from records centre to Archives is that used in France. Records centre staff prepare a list (*bordereau de versement*), in duplicate, of the documents which are to be transferred. One copy of this list is sent to the organization responsible for the documents, in order to obtain consent for the transfer to take place. This written consent is authority for the formal act of *versement*, which transfers responsibility for the documents from the original owner to the Direction des Archives.

The records centre normally provides transport for the removal of the documents, unless this is a responsibility of the Archives.

Conclusion

The general principles which have been stated in this manual have been related primarily to the needs of departments and agencies of central or federal governments whose records are the responsibility of a national or central archival authority. The use of records centres by organizations at lower levels of administration (regional and other local government authorities), and even by some larger non-public organizations, would follow the same lines. In general, however, records centres for such bodies would be smaller in capacity and less complex in operation. But whatever the size, and from whatever kinds of organization the papers it holds may come, the purpose of any records centre is the same: to provide, within an over-all system for control of records, economical storage for non-current papers until they can be either destroyed or transferred to the Archives.

In a few countries public archival authorities have already successfully established the use of records centres, and have achieved considerable influence, and even direct control, over the management of modern administrative records. Elsewhere, although there is no lack of understanding of the risks of failure to deal with the problems caused by the bulk of these records, progress has been slow and often confined to small-scale experiments. The greatest hindrance to progress is often the difficulty of convincing governments or other relevant authorities of the considerable benefits to administrators, archivists and historians which arise from proper control of retirement, storage and disposal.

For this reason an attempt has been made in the preceding chapters not only to outline some of the practical requirements of the records centre, but also to emphasize arguments which can be used to promote policies of records control. The authors have drawn for this purpose both on their own experiences and those of archivists and records managers in countries other than their own; and they have therefore considered it useful to append the text of the questionnaire which was sent to a number of public archival authorities, as well as some of the more informative replies.

To the archivist, and to potential users of documents for research purposes, the most obvious advantage of records centres, and of the general disciplines in the control of documents which must accompany their use, lies in the opportunity which it gives to improve standards of appraisal and selection and to control the flow of selected material into the Archives. It has been found, however, in most countries where records centres are already in use that the most potent argument in convincing government authorities (and particularly those responsible for the allocation of public funds) is based on the economies which can be achieved. In Canada, for example, there is an estimated saving of $3.65 for storage costs of each cubic foot moved to a records centre; and in the United States a saving of $4.33 for a cubic foot. Such direct comparisons of storage costs would not in all countries show economies of this high order; but in most cases consideration of the wider effects of a retirement and disposal system based on a records centre would show substantial long-term savings. In this way it can be shown that intervention by the archival authority in these matters can yield great benefits to the administration at large as well as to the Archives and the future needs of historical research.

It is obvious that the full benefit of the methods and procedures with which this manual has been concerned will be obtained only if they are applied uniformly and without exception to all organizations for whose records an archival authority is responsible. Exceptions will lead to inadequate control of selection and disposal, the proliferation of intermediate records stores, and the perpetuation of all the dangers which the system is intended to overcome. It is therefore essential for archival authorities to progress as quickly as possible from the limited initial experiments which normally introduce any new policy to a situation in which the responsibilities of the Archives and government departments are clearly defined by legislation or other regulation. Only in this way can a system of records management which is based on the use of a records centre be fully effective.

The authors are convinced that a solution of the problems of dealing with very large quantities of modern administrative records, which takes equal account of the needs of the organizations which produce the papers on the one hand and of historical research on the other, can be reached only by the application of the general principles they have described here. They will have achieved their limited aims in presenting this manual if it leads more countries to consider these problems and to resolve them.

Appendixes

I   Questionnaire sent to the public archival authorities of various countries

GENERAL PRINCIPLES

1. Can you define broadly any principles and practices which are applied in your country to government records which have ceased to have their most active administrative use but which have to be retained for a period of time before either destruction or transfer to the Archives? If so, please define.
2. What in your opinion is the value of these principles and practices?
3. Is any system which deals with these problems based on legislation or other formal regulation? If so, please annex the text to your reply.
4. Are procedures of the kind described above applied to:
   (a) records of all departments and agencies of central government?
   (b) records of only some departments and agencies of central government?
   (c) records of State governments (in countries with a federal system)?
   (d) records of all or some regional, municipal and other government authorities?

RECORDS CENTRES

1. Do you have in your country one or more records centres which are separate from the Archives; or is part of the Archives building set aside for the storage of non-current papers transferred from agencies to await appraisal, weeding, destruction or transfer to the Archives?
2. Give details of any records centre(s) in your country, stating in each case whether it is responsible for the papers:
   (a) of all departments and agencies of central government;
   (b) of only some departments or agencies of central government, or only one of them;
   (c) of State governments (in countries with a federal system);
   (d) of all or some regional, municipal and other government authorities.
3. What in your opinion is the best solution:
   (a) a single records centre devoted to records of all government departments and other administrative bodies?

(b) several records centres each for the common use of a number of government departments or other administrative bodies?

(c) one records centre for each kind of administrative authority.

4. Who is responsible for administering records centre(s) in your country: the Archives, or the administrative body which transfers records there?

5. Which government department or other authority is responsible for the budget for construction and equipment of the records centre(s)?

LOCATION OF RECORDS CENTRES

1. Where are records centres sited in your country?
   (a) in cities?
   (b) in suburbs?
   (c) in the country or in small towns away from the administrative centre? How far from the administrative centre?

2. In relation to the chosen site, what are the problems of communication or liaison with the transferring agencies? And how are such problems resolved?

3. What in your opinion are the kinds of location to be avoided in planning a records centre?

STRUCTURE AND EQUIPMENT OF RECORDS CENTRES

1. Have you used existing buildings which were erected for other purposes?

2. If so, what arrangements did you make to convert these buildings for use as a records centre?

3. If you have constructed new buildings, what building materials were used? What architectural design was used? (If possible, please annex plans, etc.)

4. How is the storage accommodation arranged? On how many floors or levels?

5. What kinds of shelving are used? Of what material is the shelving made? What is the total storage capacity (in linear or cubic metres or feet) in the records centre(s)?

6. What working space has been provided for the reception of transferred records, for work on weeding records, etc.?

7. What space has been provided for administrative offices, etc.?

8. What steps have you taken to assure the security of the buildings and of the papers stored there (i.e. protection against fire, theft, unauthorized access to documents, etc.)?

9. What means of internal transportation of papers do you use (hand trolleys, electrically-driven trolleys, mechanical handling systems, etc.)?

10. Has air-conditioning been installed in the records centre, or any part of it?

11. Has any photographic copying equipment been installed? For what purpose?

STAFF EMPLOYED IN THE RECORDS CENTRE

1. What is the total staff employed in the centre(s) as:
   (a) management staff?
   (b) other staff, of all grades, employed in work on the records?
2. Do you have a class of officials specially employed for management of records centres?
3. If not, are these responsible for the centres' members of the staff of the Archives, and are they professional archivists; or are they members of the staffs of the administrative agencies or authorities which use the centres?
4. Is the staff which is employed on the records wholly or partly on the staff of the Archives; or are they wholly or partly detached from the agencies, etc., which use the centres?
5. In your opinion which of the above arrangements provides the best method of staffing?

TREATMENT OF PAPERS IN THE RECORDS CENTRE

1. *Transfer*
   (a) In what circumstances are papers transferred to the records centre?
   (b) According to what criteria? (If these criteria consider storage costs in relation to such factors as the frequency of the need of the transferring agency to refer to the papers, etc., please give as much detail as practicable.)
   (c) Are the criteria for transferring papers to a records centre, and other regulations for its use, embodied in any formal rules? If so, please annex a copy to your reply.
   (d) Are these criteria decided only by the transferring agencies, etc., only by the Archives, or jointly by the various agencies and the Archives?
   (e) Which of the above is in your opinion the best way of deciding criteria?
   (f) Do you ask agencies to send with the papers being transferred some kind of check-list, either detailed or in summary form?
   (g) Are such lists checked on arrival of the papers at the records centre? How?
   (h) After transfer, to what extent are papers to which it is necessary for the transferring agency to refer:
   temporarily returned to the transferring agency?
   examined in the records centre to avoid the need to remove papers from the centre?
   photocopied in the records centre to avoid the need to remove papers from the centre?
2. *Weeding*
   (a) How is weeding carried out on records which have been transferred to the records centre?
   (b) What criteria are applied to the weeding of these records?

(c) Have you established a system of Disposal Lists or Schedules which define retention periods for different classes of papers and give disposal instructions?

(d) If so, do these Disposal Lists cover only papers which have been moved to a records centre, or do they (or separate Disposal Lists) cover also papers which are not moved to the centre?

(e) Are copies of Disposal Lists distributed to all transferring agencies, etc.?

3. *Classification*

(a) Do the papers transferred to the records centre receive a classification which is different from that which they had in the originating agency? Or are they kept in the order in which they were received so long as they remain in the records centre, leaving it to the Archives eventually to apply their own methods of classification which have the purpose of facilitating historical research?

(b) What kinds of means of reference are made in the records centre: catalogues, lists, card-indexes, etc.?

(c) Are these means of reference kept only for administrative use, or are they used also by searchers (other than the staff of transferring agencies) who are admitted to the centre to work on some of the papers there? (If research workers are not admitted to the records centre, please say so; and explain if any other arrangements are made to give them access to any documents stored there.)

4. *Destruction of valueless papers*

(a) What methods or devices do you use to destroy papers which have no longer any value?

(b) Have the transferring agencies, etc., a right to control destruction of papers which they have transferred?

(c) How do they exercise this right?

5. *Transfer to the Archives*

(a) What procedures are used for the transfer to the Archives of those papers in records centres which are recognized to have historical value?

(b) How old are the records when they are transferred to the Archives? Are there any precise rules on this subject?

THE PROBLEM OF DOCUMENTS IN 'NEW' FORMS

1. Are there already in your records centre(s) some records which are not in conventional (paper) form but in other forms (audio-visual records, magnetic tapes, etc.)?

2. Whether or not you have records of these kinds please indicate if in your opinion it is necessary to consider their treatment now?

2a Cité Interministérielle des Archives, Fontainebleau (France)
General plan

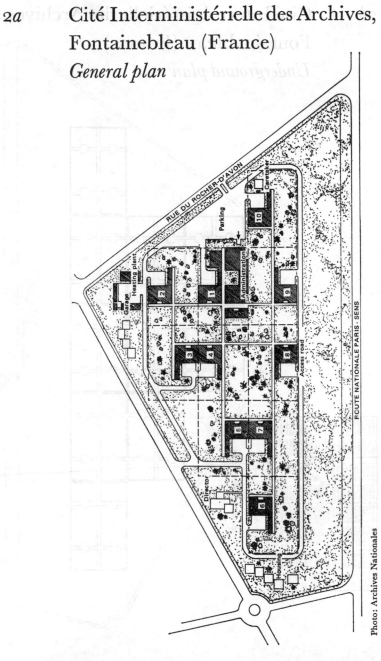

Photo: Archives Nationales

61

2b   Cité Interministérielle des Archives, Fontainebleau (France)
Underground plan

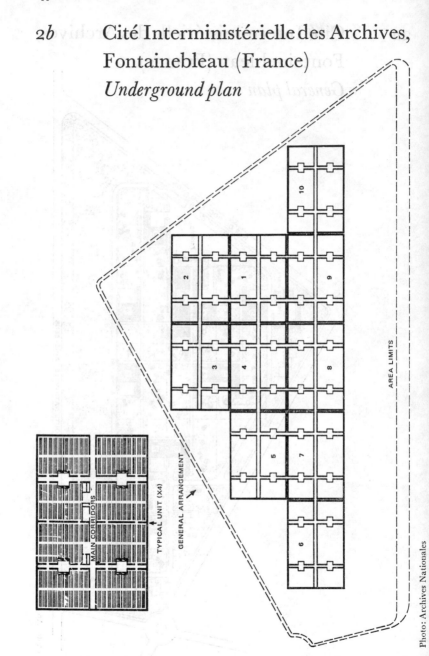

2c Cité Interministérielle des Archives,
Fontainebleau (France)
Section of one unit

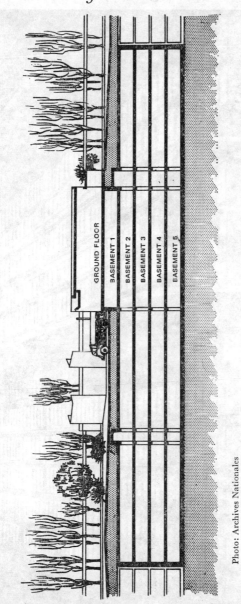

GROUND FLOOR

BASEMENT 1

BASEMENT 2

BASEMENT 3

BASEMENT 4

BASEMENT 5

Photo: Archives Nationales

3 Racking in the Intermediate Repository at Hayes (United Kingdom)

4   Federal Records Center facility standards (United States)[1]

For nearly twenty-five years the growth of the 'records centre' as a facility for storing, processing and disposing of records not active enough to be kept in high-cost office space and equipment, has become a necessary adjunct to the successful management of records.

The right kind of building is a 'must' for economical operation. The following elements are considered of major importance in achieving the purpose of records centres:

1. Centre structures should be simple in style and functional in arrangement. Permanent type construction is essential. Concrete block with brick façade lends itself to this kind of construction especially well. The site should be of sufficient size to include space for paved parking and vehicle manoeuvring, and should be near a main arterial highway. In general, one-storey buildings should be provided for centres requiring less than 1 million cubic foot records storage capacity. Two-storey buildings are desirable for centres requiring 1 million or more cubic foot records capacity, provided the site will lend itself to the use of trucking docks at both levels. Multiple-storey existing buildings must be considered when their location and physical characteristics permit safe and economical operation and the cost of new construction can be avoided.

2. Centre buildings should be individual structures, sufficiently separate from other buildings and external hazards to insure a high degree of safety from fire, flood, and other possible disaster.

3. Centres should normally be sole occupants of their buildings. Where they share space with other occupants, adequate precautions should be taken to eliminate fire hazards by separation fire walls and by other protective measures.

4. A uniformly distributed live load of 300 pounds is required, except for office areas. Live load for roof depends on the geographical location.

5. Whenever practicable, ceiling height throughout the records storage

1. Washington, D.C., National Archives and Records Service, 1970.

area should provide at least 16 feet of stacking height completely clear of ducts, pipes, etc., providing necessary clear space (usually 18 inches) beneath sprinkler heads.

6. Columns should be arranged to avoid the need for expensive roof trussing, yet permit optimum stack space use by elimination of only one standard 30 × 42 inch shelving unit per column.

7. A four-hour fire resistive vault, mercantile type, for storage of security classified records, as well as temperature and humidity controlled space for storage of permanent records, magnetic tapes and photographic film, is required.

8. Loading docks should be similar to those in any first-class warehouse, with sufficient space to accommodate simultaneous loading and unloading operations for at least two trailer-type trucks. They should be in enclosable (interior) space and be equipped with automatic levelling plates.

9. The general scope and requirements for the electrical facilities which should be provided include:
    primary electric power supply;
    transformation from the above to 208/120 volts, 3-phase, 4-wire;
    fire-alarm system;
    intrusion and security systems;
    smoke detection system;
    lighting circuits and fixtures;
    air-conditioning (office spaces);
    temperature and humidity controls.

10. Centres require the following minimum standards for illumination at 3 feet height above floor level:
    storage space: fluorescent (direct), 25 foot-candles;
    office space: fluorescent (semi-direct), 50 foot-candles.

11. Office areas, vault and the archival storage area should be air-conditioned. In addition, the vault and archives spaces should have the following temperature and humidity standards to meet the requirements for storage of special materials:
    temperature: 74° ± 4° Fahrenheit;
    relative humidity 50 per cent ± 2 per cent.
    If the humidity control can provide against sharp fluctuations in moisture content, the variation can be ± 4 per cent. Other stack areas should be ventilated by a fresh-air forced-ventilation system (heavy duty).

12. The entrance vestibule should be equipped with standard built-in exhibit cases.

13. All facilities shall comply with the criteria listed below with respect to fire-safety. In addition, the lower storey of any two-storey facility and all portions of any buildings higher than two storeys shall comply with the requirements for Type A fire-resistive construction. The detailed description of Type A fire-resistive construction is contained in Chapter 2–3 of the GSA handbook, *Building Firesafety Criteria* (PBS P 5920.9).

Area

There is no fire-safety limit on the total building area. The facility, how ever, shall be separated by fire walls into individual records storage areas not exceeding 40,000 square feet each.

Fire walls

All walls separating records storage areas from other portions of the building shall be four-hour fire-resistive fire walls. In addition to fire resistance, all fire walls shall be structurally sound, capable of standing impact and imposed loads, if severe fire exposure would cause collapse of the framing members on one side of the wall. All openings in fire walls, shall be protected by Class 'A' fire doors on each side of the fire wall. No ducts shall pass through fire walls that separate two records storage areas. Properly protected duct passes may be established between records storage areas and corridors or office areas. Fire walls should be erected preferably without expansion joints. If expansion joints are essential, they shall be protected to their full height with No. 10 iron astragals lapping the opening on each side of the wall.

Columns

Building columns located within the records storage area, shall be two-hour fire-resistive, from floor to the point where they meet the roof framing system.

Roof

Roofs shall be noncombustible. If framing is simple, no fire resistance is required. Any continuous members or other framing systems having a direct effect on more than one structural bay shall be of two-hour fire resistance. No portion of the roof framing system shall pass across a fire wall.

Exits

Exits from all facilities shall comply with the requirements of Chapter 4-3 of the GSA handbook, *Building Firesafety Criteria* (PBS P 5920.9).

Light fixtures

Light fixtures for stack areas shall not be more than 9 inches wide including the maximum width of the reflector. The fixture shall be of all metal construction and shall be equipped with thermally protected ballasts. The lowest point on any fixture shall be at least 12 inches higher than the top of the highest record storage.

Air-handling

The air-handling system shall be designed so that it can be manually converted to total outside air and used for emergency smoke removal. All ducts shall be steel. Ducts may be above or below the roof level, but shall be co-ordinated with the sprinkler system to maintain full distribution and required clearances from maximum records storage height.

Heating

Any furnaces or boilers shall be separated from the records storage by a four-hour fire wall, with no openings directly from the furnace or boiler room to the records storage areas. No open flame (oil or gas) equipment shall be used in any records area.

Service aisles

The stack arrangement shall be such that there will be no dead-end aisles. Where stacking runs perpendicular to the wall, it shall terminate at least 18 inches from the wall.

Loading docks

Loading docks shall be separated from records areas by four-hour fire walls with proper fire door protection and by two-hour fire partitions from any other portions of the building.

Security vaults

Security vault walls and roof shall be four-hour fire-resistive. Fire doors shall be as required for other records areas and shall be separate from security doors.

Automatic sprinkler protection

All records storage areas, security vaults, loading docks, or corridors, offices, service areas, or other space within the general records storage area, shall be sprinkler protected. The only exception to sprinkler protection within the records area shall be electrical wire closets or transformer vaults in separate fire-resistive enclosures. Sprinkler heads shall be rated at 212°F. Systems shall be hydraulically designed to operate at a static pressure of 80 to 100 psi at the sprinkler riser; and to deliver a uniform minimum discharge density of 0.30 gallons per square foot per minute over 2,500 square feet, and 0.20 gallons per square foot per minute over 5,000 square feet. Maximum spacing of sprinkler heads shall be 10 feet and positioning of heads above floor shall be such as to provide complete unobstructed coverage with at least 18 inches clearance from highest stacking height (from top of highest stored materials).

Water supply

If the water supply for the records centre is of a design whereby both sprinkler protection and fire hydrants are taken from the same source, the water-supply system shall be capable of delivering not less than 1,600 gallons per minute at 65 psi; 2,800 gallons per minute at 30 psi, and 3,000 gallons per minute at 20 psi. The system shall be capable of delivering the maximum capacity requirement (3,000 gallons per minute) for a period of at least three hours.

A dependable water supply virtually free of interruption is required. This will frequently, but not universally, require a two-source system. A single-feed main from the public water system would not be considered a dependable source. Two feeds from different points in the public system would be considered satisfactory, if dependable facility fire pumps are provided. An on-site reservoir with both electric motor and internal-combustion-engine-driven pumps is another example of a single, but adequately dependable supply. Any two-source system with sufficient pressure and capacity in each source is, of course, also satisfactory.

Interior hose stations

Interior hose stations connected to the sprinkler systems and conforming to the requirements of National Fire Protection Association Standard No. 13 shall be provided in such a manner that any point in the stack area can be reached by a 50-foot hose stream from a 100-foot hose lay. Each hose station shall be provided with a rack and reel capable of holding 100 feet of 1½ inch rubber or latex lined hose. The hose and a shut-off type nozzle shall be provided from Federal Supply Schedule after completion of the structure.

Fire hydrants

Fire hydrants shall be located so that each entrance, or other access to the records centre that could be used by firefighters, shall be within 250 feet of a fire hydrant. All hydrants shall be at least 50 feet away from the building wall and adjacent to a roadway usable by fire apparatus.

Alarm system

All records storage areas only, shall be provided with an ion chamber, early-warning type fire detection system. Detectors shall be located on a maximum spacing of 1,000 square foot coverage per detector, with such additional detectors or arrangement as required by the established air-flow pattern. The early warning detection system shall be entirely separate in its wiring and controls from any other system. Provision shall be made, however, for an appropriate transmitter (or other device) to transmit the signal across the building fire alarm system, indicating detection. Depending on the arrangement and lay of the building, multiple transmitters may be necessary to indicate zoning or location of the alarm source.

It is desirable that the specification for the ion chamber system state that the indicated 1,000 square foot spacing is maximum and that the contractor is responsible for providing a system that will detect a fire ignited in 1 pound of burning shreaded paper contained in a 12-inch diameter wire mesh cylinder placed anywhere in the records storage area within 120 seconds of a simple match ignition. The specification should also require that the detectors shall also operate without more than one false alarm per year for the entire installation, at the sensitivity required to meet the detection requirements. Also, detectors shall not require servicing or cleaning more than once each year and that such servicing or cleaning shall be capable of accomplishment in not over 120 seconds by one man not including time to reach the detector. Any dismantling of the detector for cleaning shall not require tools. Detectors shall not be sensitive to humidity change. Acceptance of detectors shall be subject to proof test by the prescribed fire after racks are installed, but before any records are placed in the building.

The building shall be provided with a manual, shunt, non-interfering, coded, general, fire-alarm system. Fire-alarm striking stations (boxes) shall be located at each of the exits from stack areas and each of the exits from the building. No other fire-alarm boxes shall be located in stack areas. The fire-alarm system shall be provided with central station service or other automatic means of notifying the municipal fire department.

Each sprinkler system shall be provided with an alarm check valve, with a water motor gong, a retard chamber and a pressure-type electric actuator for a water-flow alarm to be transmitted over the manual fire-alarm system.

All water-control valves on the sprinkler systems, or other principal valves on the fire protection system, shall be provided with tamper supervision. Tamper supervision shall be separate from the manual fire alarm system.

Electrical equipment

No transformers, regardless of size, except thermally-protected devices included in fluorescent light ballasts, shall be permitted within the stack areas. All electric control boxes and light switches shall be located at the main entrance to the stack area.

Emergency vents

Emergency heat and smoke vents shall not be provided.

First aid firefighting equipment

Water-type fire extinguishers (2½ gallon stored pressure type), shall be provided at each fire-alarm striking station.

5   Regulations of the Dépôt de Préarchivage of the Cité Administrative, Melun (France)

1. There shall be set up in the Cité Administrative, Melun, à *dépôt de préarchivage* for the storing of documents which are no longer in current use in the offices of the Cité.
2. This depository shall be placed under the responsibility of the Director of the Departmental Archives. The Archives of France shall provide technical assistance in the running of the said depository.
3. Personnel, whether supplied by the Directorate of the Archives of France or by the Cité Administrative, shall be placed under the authority of the Director of the Departmental Archives.
4. Fittings and equipment expenses and operating costs shall be borne by the Cité Administrative and financed from the general operating budget of the Cité, being, as in the case of other expenditure, prorated according to the surface area of the offices equipped.
5. Access to documents shall be given freely to the depositing agencies and, with their authorization, to other services, either by making use of the depository's transport service or in the depository's reading-room. When appropriate, it shall also be granted to research workers, until the date of free access to all categories of documents is reached.
6. Transfers shall be made in conformity with the decree of 21 July 1936 and transfer forms shall be issued in respect of them. In principle, in order that optimum use may be made of the capacity of the premises, the system of continuous classification shall be adopted, instead of each agency having a separate sector reserved for it.
7. Eliminations shall be made in accordance with the procedure in force and, in every case, subject to the approval of the archives service.
8. The archives service shall be responsible for preparing the necessary card-indexes, lists and inventories, and for classifying, appraising and eliminating the files transferred. Documents which are to be preserved for an indeterminate length of time and which have been duly classified may, once their storage in a locality close to the offices is no longer necessary for convenience of operation, be transferred to Departmental Archives.

(14 February 1973)

6   Specimens of disposal schedules

(a) Disposal lists of official documents, Ministry of Agriculture, Fisheries and Food (United Kingdom)

Class of document	Disposal instruction
A. Registered papers	
Files in the following series containing material likely to be of value as a precedent, of historical or legal importance, useful for social or economic research or relating to policy or procedure	To be considered for permanent preservation
B.A. Livestock subsidies	
1. Accounts and finance:	
(a) Administration costs; estimates and costings; financial arrangements and proposals	Retain for second review
(b) Annual returns of expenditure; vote code lists	Destroy 6 years after the end of the relevant financial year
(c) Annual review	
(d) Consolidated expenditure in the United Kingdom	
(e) Decimal currency	
(f) Extra statutory and *ex-gratia* payments	Retain for second review
(g) Mechanization of payments; general arrangements	
(h) Payments of subsidies and grants; payments for livestock slaughtered under Foot and Mouth Disease Orders	Destroy 6 years after the end of the financial year of payment
(i) Recovery of overpayments	Destroy 5 years after last action

Class of document	Disposal instruction
2. Audit	See General Section (page 23, item 1)
3. Commissions, committees and councils	See General Section (page 23, item 2)
4. Conferences, congresses and conventions	See General Section (page 23, item 3)
5. Grants and subsidies: (a) Acreage limitations; basis of calculations	Retain for second review
(b) Applications: (i) requests for forms; (ii) appeals against non-acceptance decisions	Destroy 5 years after last action

(b) Archives appraisal schedule of the departmental offices of the Ministry of Agriculture (France)

Nature of documents	Length of time in the agencies or offices concerned	Subsequently stored in the Departmental Archives
Protective forests, fixation of dunes, management of catchment basins Files for each category		
(a) construction files	10 years after final acceptance	All documents
(b) files of work	10 years after final acceptance	All documents (or sample selection in the event of their being too voluminous)
Deforestation management Regulations	As long as these remain in force	All documents
Statistical reports, general files	10 years	All documents
Summary records of deforestation operations	10 years	All documents
Individual files on operations	5 years after final acceptance	Sample
Registers of declarations	10 years after closing date	All documents

Nature of documents	Length of time in the agencies or offices concerned	Subsequently stored in the Departmental Archives
Erosion control and restoration of mountain lands		
Regulations	As long as these remain in force	All documents
Reports, statistics, general files	10 years	All documents
Announcements concerning boundaries of restoration areas	As long as the texts remain in force	All documents
Records of work	10 years	All documents
Accounting registers	10 years	All documents
Individual files on operations	5 years after final acceptance	Sample
Control of forest fires		
Regulations	As long as these remain in force	All documents
Reports, statistics, general files	10 years	All documents
Register of forest fires	5 years	All documents
Individual files	5 years	Preserve files on the major fires
Loans made by the National Forest Fund for the purchase of equipment	5 years	Destroy